SCOTT FORESMAN

SiDEWALKS

Treasures

Program Authors

Connie Juel, Ph.D.

Jeanne R. Paratore, Ed.D.

Deborah Simmons, Ph.D.

Sharon Vaughn, Ph.D.

ISBN: 0-328-21429-9

Copyright © 2008 Pearson Education, Inc.

PEARSON

Scott Foresman

2 3 4 5 6 7 8 9 10 V003 12 11 10 09 08 07 06

Editorial Offices: Glenview, Illinois • Parsippany, New Jersey • New York, New York
Sales Offices: Boston, Massachusetts • Duluth, Georgia • Glenview, Illinois
Coppell, Texas • Sacramento, California • Mesa, Arizona

UNIT 4 Contents

Treasures

Surprising Treasures

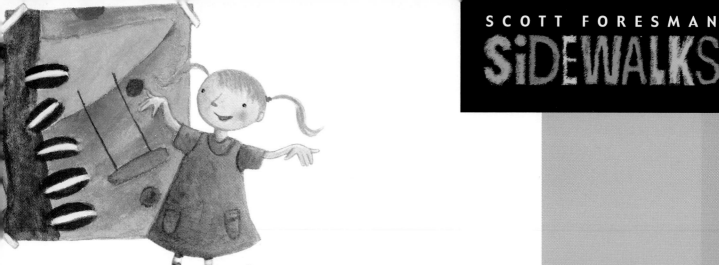

SCOTT FORESMAN
SIDEWALKS

Treasures to Share

Contents

Surprising Treasures

See page 33 for My New Words and Pictionary!

Surprise!

Look up at the sky. How big it is! How black it is!

See the stars. See them shine.
See what the stars make.
Surprise!

Spot the nest in that tree. A chick rests in that nest. It will try to fly.

Will the chick fall? Surprise!
It will not. It can fly and fly.

It was wet. But now it is dry.

The sun shines in the sky. It makes red, blue, and green.
Surprise!

Be still! Ty is home! Ty can spy his pals. He can see their feet.

Some other pals hide by Mom. "Surprise, Ty!" his pals are yelling with smiles.

What Is in the Box?

by Fay Marina

What can go in a box? Look at its size. How big is it? How small is it? Look at its shape. How tall is it? How wide is it?

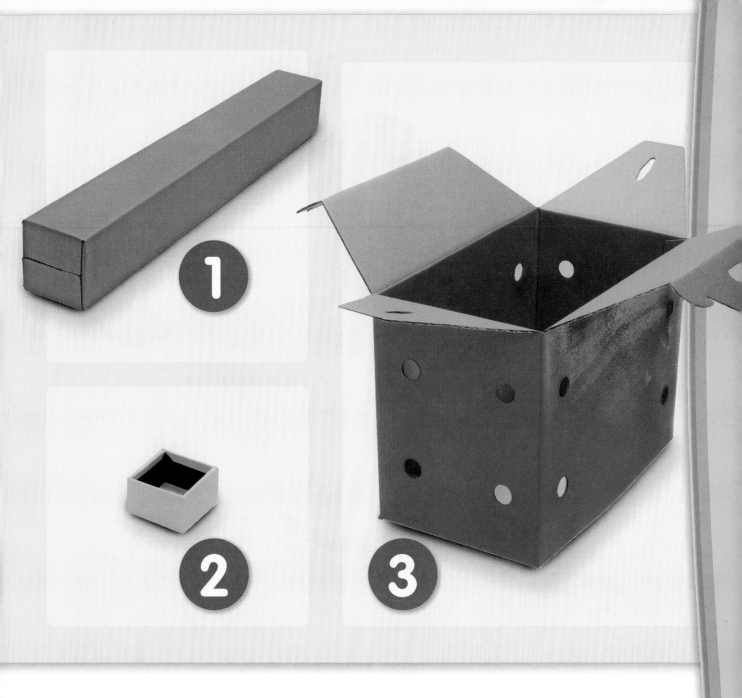

What can go in box 1? What can go in box 2? What can go in box 3?

This box is tall and skinny. Can a fluffy puppy fit in it? Danny can fit his lucky bat in it. The bat is tall and skinny like this box.

Name some other stuff that can fit in this box. Try!

This box is small. What can fit in a small box? This box has a penny in it. The penny is small like the box.

Try and name some other stuff that can fit in this box.

This box is big. It has holes. It has a big, fluffy bunny and a small, funny bunny in it. They hop, hop in their box.

Try and name some others that can go in this box.

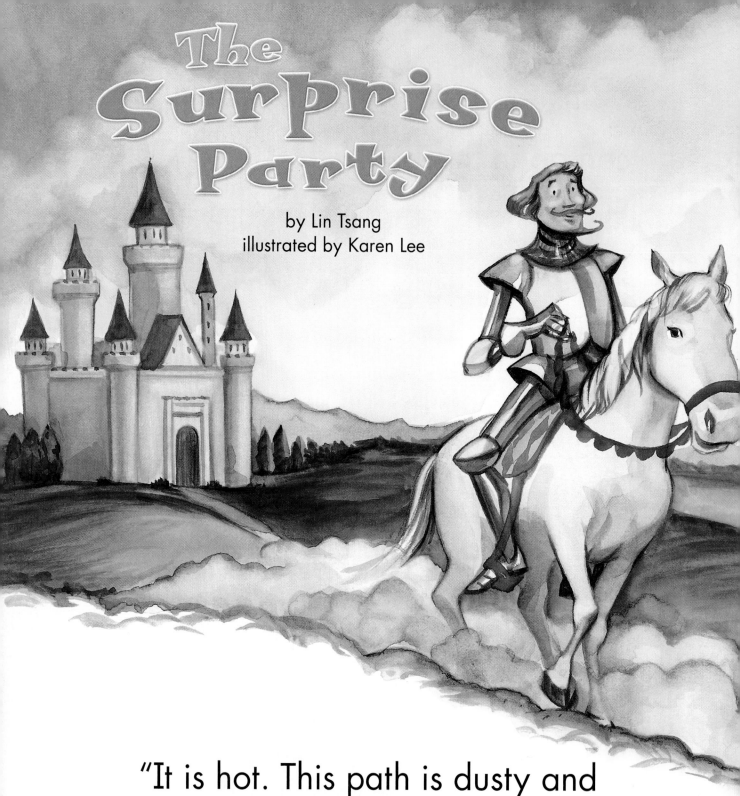

The Surprise Party

by Lin Tsang
illustrated by Karen Lee

"It is hot. This path is dusty and bumpy. But the sky is sunny. Trot fast, Trusty, trot fast," said Sir Prize. "I must try to see Queen Wendy."

They rode and rode on that dusty and bumpy path.

But Sir Prize needed sleep. He
made camp by a big lake. The sky
had lots and lots of stars.

When the sun came up, Sir Prize
woke up and left his camp.

He rode and rode. Then he saw
some men walking and talking.

"When is their party in that big hall?" one man asked.

"It is at five," the other man said. "We can not be late."

"The party must be for Queen Wendy. It must be a surprise. We, too, can not be late. Trot fast, Trusty, trot fast," said Sir Prize.

"I must stop and get a gift. My, my! How fine this is! I will get this green pin. Queen Wendy will like this fine, green pin," said Sir Prize.

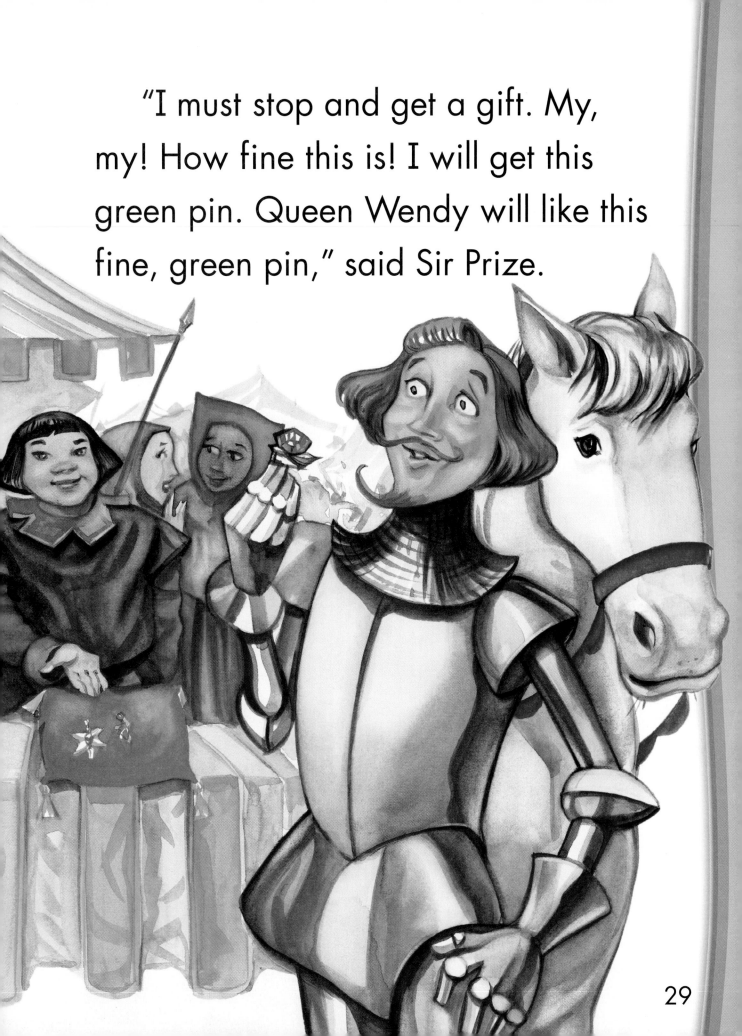

"This is the big hall," Sir Prize said.
He peeked in.

30

Then Queen Wendy and the others yelled, "Surprise, Sir Prize!" And that did surprise Sir Prize! The party was for him!

Riddle Time

I like to run.

I like to lick.

I would like to fetch a stick.

What am I?

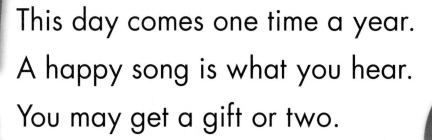

This day comes one time a year.

A happy song is what you hear.

You may get a gift or two.

What happy day is it for you?

Answers: a dog; a birthday

32

My New Words

how   Tell me **how** to win a prize.
How long will it take?

other   Pick one size and not the
other. The **other** sizes
do not fit.

some   **Some** kids like to swim.
Some don't.

their   They clapped **their** hands.

Pictionary

party

stars

Contents

Surprising Treasures

Make Something Special

You can make fun stuff with old things. Use any odds and ends.

Pick small things such as clips, pins, and buttons.

You can get magnets and make them cute. You can use small stones. You can use shells. Stick them on the magnets.

Hang up notes with cute new magnets.

You can make a bank with a can.
Ask Dad to cut a hole in its lid. Stick
odds and ends on the can.

40

Drop in five dimes and one penny.
Clink, clink, clink, clink, clink! Plunk!

What will you do with all these new things?

Friends will like them. Try it!

42

43

The Fish Tank

by Angela Lamb

Jenny thinks, "I will fix up our small fish tank."

She sets up the fish tank. Jenny
drops small stones in the tank. Clink,
clank, clink, clank.

Fish need water. Jenny fills the tank with water. Glub, blub, glub, blub.

Jenny can pick any fish she likes. Jenny sees one guppy she likes. Then she sees five others she likes. She gets all six fish.

Fish need to eat. Jenny gets
fish flakes.

Fish like to swim by plants. Jenny sees plants and a small chest. Jenny brings these things home.

Jenny drops the chest in the water.
She sees it sink.

Will plants sink? They do not sink.
Jenny keeps them in place with stones.

Jenny drops in six fish. Plink, plunk, plink, plunk, plink, plunk. "Swim, fish, swim."

Jenny thinks, "Our fish are the best! These six fish got a new tank. And they got a new friend—me!"

The Picture

by Tom King • illustrated by Susan Mitchell

Frank made a picture. He hung it
up. His friend Mandy came to see it.
"This is my new picture," he said.

"I think it is a wing," Mandy said.
"It seems like a big wing."

Then Denny came to see it.

"This is my picture," Frank said.

"I think it is a swing," Denny said.
"It is like our pink swing at home."

Then Sky came to see it.

"This is my picture," Frank said.

"It looks like five skunks on a tree trunk," Sky said. "Yes! It must be five skunks on a tree trunk!"

"Thank you all," said Frank.
"Mandy sees a big wing. Denny sees
a pink swing. Sky sees five skunks on
a tree trunk.

"I did not put any of those things in my picture. But if you see them, that is fine with me!"

THUMB FUN

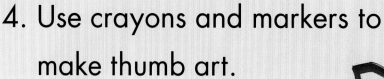

Directions

1. Dip your thumb in a little paint.

2. Press your thumb on paper.

3. Wash your hands.

4. Use crayons and markers to make thumb art.

What will you make?

62

My New Words

any	Do you have **any** cans left?
friend	I like my **friend**.
new	This hat is old and not **new**.
our	**Our** class has fish in a tank.

Pictionary

picture

trunk —

Contents

Surprising Treasures

See page 85 for My New Words and Pictionary!

Treasures in the Earth

What is inside Earth? We will see.

Metal is inside Earth. What can we make with metal? We can make planes and ships. We can make pots and pans.

Salt can be inside. What must be done to get that salt from Earth? Deep tunnels are dug to get that salt.

Fossils can be inside rocks. Fossils let us know that plants were here. We can see something from the past again in these fossils.

Gems can be inside. Gems are fancy stones. We can use gems on rings and pins.

Now we know some things that we get from Earth. Were any of these a surprise?

Gems

by Michael Stevens

See all these stones. These
stones came from inside Earth. All
these stones are called gems.

  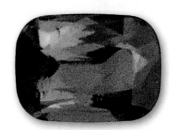

Gems are not all the same color. Gems can be red. Gems can be white. Gems can be pink. Look at these gems. Name the colors.

Gems can be small. Gems can be big. But there are not huge gems. Look at these. Pick one you like.

Stones can have bumps, gashes, and odd shapes. These stones will be cut. Then someone will make them shine. It takes lots of skill for this to be done.

In this place anyone can hunt for gems. Just dig them up. You do not need to dig deep. They can be on top.

This kid wishes he had a gem. Some who hunt are lucky and get gems. Some are not. Good luck!

Bones to Pick

by Ronald Buescher
illustrated by Rémy Simard

Deen rushes inside. He takes
something from his backpack.
"Dad, do you know what this is?"

Dad grabs his glasses. "I think it is a fossil. I think it is an old bone."

Dad wants to see if the bone matches bones on the Web page.

"Are we done yet?" asks Deen. "Yes, Deen. This bone is not a match. We will try again. I know someone we can ask."

Dad and Deen went into a big
lab. Big boxes and small boxes were
filled with bones.

Deen passes the bone he has to a man. "Can you tell me what this is?" asks Deen.

"Let me see." The man smiles. "It is five inches long. It is like this leg bone! It is from a small one like this. This is a fine fossil!"

Deen feels lucky. He smiles.

Let's Dig!

Read each clue. Find the hidden treasure in the picture.

1. I am an old bone.
2. I am shiny and yellow.
3. I go on a ring.
4. There is treasure inside me.

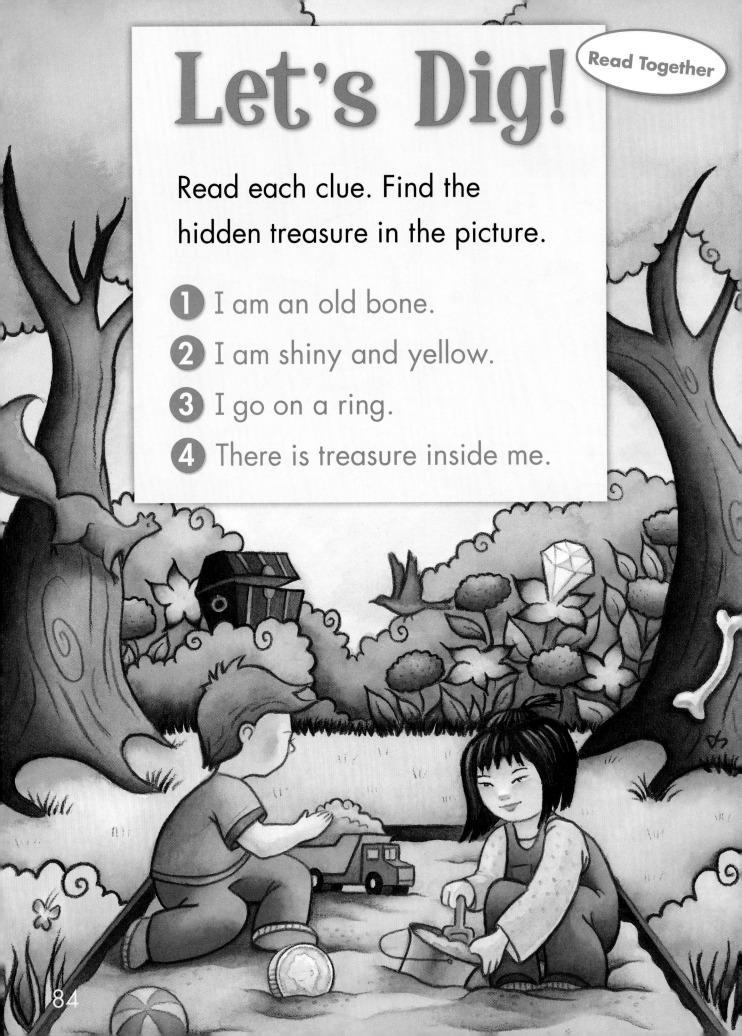

84

My New Words

again   Can you say it **again**?

done   She can swim when her homework is **done**.

gashes   **Gashes** are deep cuts. He used a knife to make **gashes** in the log.

know   I **know** the answer.

were   We **were** late and missed the class party.

Pictionary

fossil

metal

Contents

Treasures to Share

See page 109 for My New Words and Pictionary!

Special Times with Others

Times we spend with others are
the best. We meet at homes.

We smile and hug. We eat and
talk. These are fine times for all.

Every June the four of us have fun
at the shore. Mom and Dad and kids
can swim. We rest and swim and
then rest and swim more.

We hope it does not storm. If it storms, we must get off the shore.

Baseball games are fun times. This sport has three bases and a home plate. Men bat a ball and run.

We clap and yell if they score a run. We eat popcorn and hot dogs.

Time with Mom or Dad is nice.
We sit on a porch or on a deck.

We take a walk or a ride. We tell things that we are thinking.

Wave a Flag

by Ann Armelie

The U.S.A. has a big party every summer. On this date we think of our land and how it is a good place for us.

Stores close. Moms and dads do not go to their jobs. More of us can have fun.

See the U.S. flags. See red and
white lines. See white stars on blue.

The white stars stand for our 50 states. The lines stand for the 13 parts that made up this land when it was just starting.

Bands march in the U.S.A. Bands have horns, flutes, and drums. Off they march. Kids march in bands too.

We can see picnics in parks and yards. Moms and dads bring snacks. Kids bring games. We all have fun.

It gets dark. The sky has sparks
that shine. Does the sky fill with color?
Are there big pops and bangs?

Pop! Bang! Pop! Bang! Kids yell for more. Kids wave flags.

Family Tales

by Aaron Philips • illustrated by Hector Borlasca

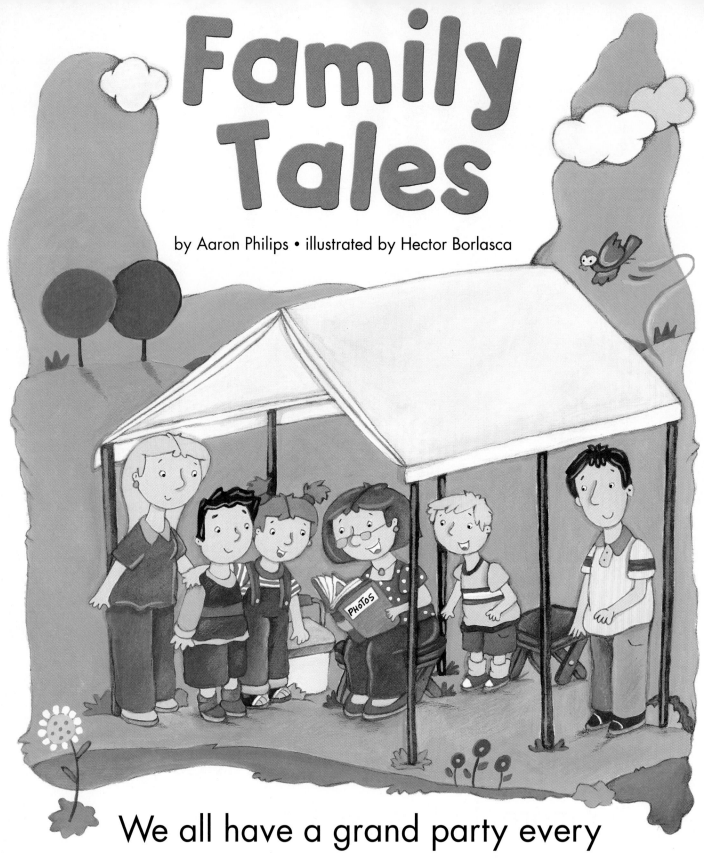

We all have a grand party every June. We talk and look at funny pictures. We tell tales.

Gram starts. "We had chores on
the farm. We picked corn. We fed
hens. One time I fell off my big horse
and broke my left arm!"

"Fishing is fun," said Dad. "One time I got four fish. Then I fell in and got all wet. My hat, my pole, and all my fish went far down the creek!"

"Baseball is for me," Mandy said. "One time I hit five home runs. They went outside the park."

Everyone does tell lots of tales!

Did You Know?

The biggest July 4 fireworks show is in New York City.

The first Thanksgiving was in 1621. It did not become a holiday until 1863—over 240 years later!

On Earth Day, some people do not use any lights, watch TV, or talk on the phone. Could you do that?

My New Words

does   **Does** she skate well?

every   **Every** child needs to bring books to class.

four   **Four** is one more than three.

off   The cat jumps **off** the bed. The radio is **off**.

Pictionary

U.S.A.

Contents

Treasures to Share

See page 135 for My New Words and Pictionary!

Treasures at Home

Are there treasures in your home? Check in this box. Is there something you forgot about?

Is it a small car? Is it a truck? Is it
this fur bunny you once curled up with?
This can be a nice treasure.

Check family snapshots. Pick one that makes you smile. Is it you and your family all together?

Is it Mom or Dad? Is it you with pets? Is it your dog or bird? What is his name? What is her name?

Check inside bags. What treasure will you see first? Is it in a box? Is it in a jar?

Is it sweet? Is it salty? Is it crunchy?
Is it yummy? Did Mom or Dad get it
for you? All these can be treasures.

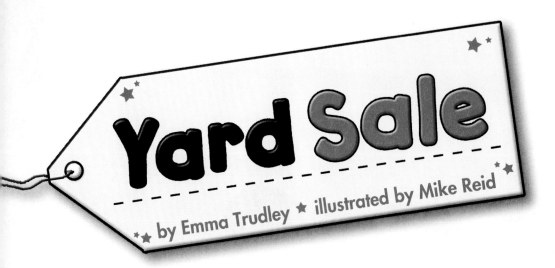

We had lots to do for the yard sale.

Running a yard sale is hard! But it is fun.

First we planned the date for the sale.

Then we made an ad.

Next my family picked things to sell. Mom had about fifty things. Tim gave shirts. Sis gave her purse. I gave my stuffed fur dog.

Then we made price tags for things. How much for this purse? What is the price for an old fur dog? We spent lots of time tagging things.

We needed to tell everyone where to go. We had fun with this job!

We had black and green and
red to do the job. It was messy.
But together we did a good job.

We put things on benches. Then it was about time for the sale to start.

At nine, moms and dads and kids started to drive up. Cars parked at the curb. Our time for sitting had passed!

More came. They shopped
and shopped. Mom was the clerk.
I helped. I sat with the cash box.

Once I asked a man, "Did you get
a treasure?" He grinned and hugged
his bag of stuff.

Running a yard sale is hard! But my family had fun together. We will plan a yard sale again next fall!

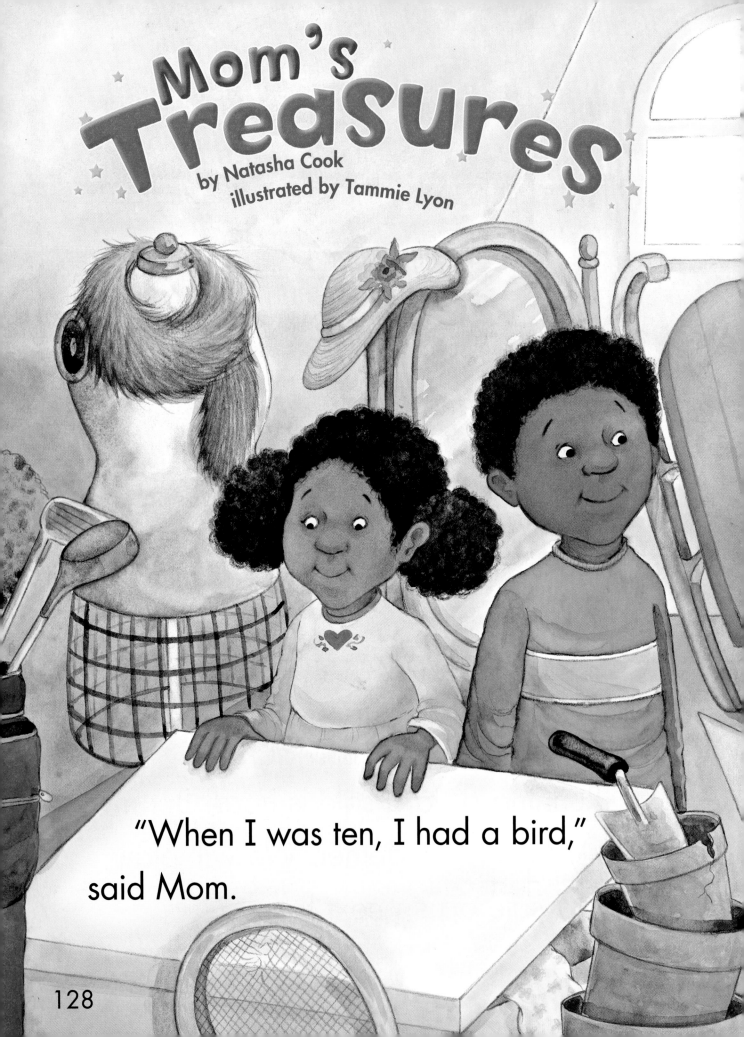

Mom's Treasures

by Natasha Cook

illustrated by Tammie Lyon

"When I was ten, I had a bird," said Mom.

"This is her cage. It is very old. I can still see my bird sitting on this perch singing tunes."

"This is my jump rope," said Mom.
"It is not that old. All my pals skipped
rope together on my sidewalk. I can
still see us jumping and grinning."

"My dad once had a tan horse,"
said Mom. "This went on her back.
It is not that old. We trotted on a
path about ten miles."

"This is very old," said Mom. "It is a churn. It turns thick milk into butter. My family has kept it all this time."

"Next week, we will go shopping for milk. Then we will use the churn and make butter together. Old things can be new again!"

Treasure

by Lee Bennett Hopkins

A rusty door key,
A part of a tool,
A dead bee I was saving
to take in to school;

A crust of pizza,
Sand from the shore,
A piece of lead pipe,
An old apple core;

My library card,
A small model rocket—
I guess it is time to clean
out my pocket.

My New Words

about   This book is **about** trains.
              About 12 cans can fit
              in the box.

family   The people who take care
              of you are your **family**.

once   **Once** means one time.
              Once is also a time
              in the past.

together Mix the milk and egg
              together.

treasures **Treasures** are things that
              are very special to you.

Pictionary

perch

Contents

136

Treasures to Share

See page 159 for My New Words and Pictionary!

Sharing with Neighbors

People need many things for jobs.
Ann will ask her pal Sammy for help.

Can she use his green rake? He's
happy to give this rake to her. She's
going to rake her yard now.

Many kids share things. Jim has big trucks and small trucks. He's happy to share.

Jim will let his pal use his trucks.
That's nice of him. This pal will share
his cars with Jim next time.

Many kids can share how to make
things. This girl likes crafts.

She can make cute things. She's telling her pals how to make these things. It's great when people share!

Great Gardens

by Dominic Lewis • illustrated by Lindy Burnett

These people share a garden. They all have homes close by. Let's take a look.

Here's a rose garden. We can see many pink and red roses.

This is Jill. She tends her rose plants. She's cutting rose stems with buds on them. They're for Jen and Nan.

Look at this! Here's a great garden.

We can see many mums.

These kids had luck with big mums
and small mums. They're happy to give
them to people.

You've seen corn in cans. But have you seen corn plants?

Corn is on tall stalks. Peel back the husks. There's corn on the cob.

People pick corn and fix it to eat.
We all like corn on the cob! It's
yummy in the tummy. It's great!

Great Helpers

by Ashanti Jones • illustrated by Bob Masheris

Sam is going to make a swing set.
"I've got lots of work," he said.
"It will take weeks to make a swing
set by myself."

"I'll ask Ben if he has a big saw."
"Yes," said Ben. "I've got two
saws. I can give you a hand. Let's
get started!"

Sam cut. Buzz! Buzz! Buzz!

Ben cut. Buzz! Buzz! Buzz!

"Now we've got to get a drill," said
Sam. "We need a drill to make holes."
"I will ask Jane," said Ben.

"Yes, I've got a drill," said Jane.
"I'll get it, and I can help too."

Sam cut. BuzZ! BuzZ! BuzZ!
Ben cut. BuzZ! BuzZ! BuzZ!
Jane drilled. Hum! Hum! Hum!

Ben and Sam cut. Buzz! Buzz! Buzz!

Jane drilled. Hum! Hum! Hum!

Ben, Sam, and Jane worked hard.

"Thanks, all!" grinned Sam. "Many people helped, and we're done at last. Kids will like this great swing set!"

Come to the
BLOCK PARTY

 When: Saturday, July 28, at 2:00 P.M.

 Where: Our Block

 What to Bring: Food to Share

 Games for All . . . . .

 Balloon Toss

 Egg Toss

Treasure Hunt

 Big Bike Parade

Would you like to go to this block party?

My New Words

give   If you **give** me something, you let me have it.

great   Something that is **great** is very good or important.

many   **Many** means a large number or a lot.

people **People** are men, women, and children.

Pictionary

drill

husk

stalk

Acknowledgments

Poetry

134 "Treasure" by Lee Bennett Hopkins, from *Good Rhymes, Good Times*. Originally published as "Digging for Treasure" in *Humpty Dumpty's Magazine*. Copyright © 1972, 1995 by Lee Bennett Hopkins.

Illustrations

4, 22–31 Karen Lee; **5–13** Laura Ovresat; **34, 54–61** Susan Mitchell; **64, 78–83** Remy Simard; **84** Dena Sieferling; **86, 104–107, 134–136** Hector Borlasca; **102, 111, 144–148** Lindy Burnett; **107, 137, 150–157** Robert Masheris; **110, 128–130–133** Tammie Lyon; **111, 118–127** Mick Reid; **118** Gladys Rosa-Mendoza; **137–143** Elizabeth Allen

Photographs

Every effort has been made to secure permission and provide appropriate credit for photographic material. The publisher deeply regrets any omission and pledges to correct errors called to its attention in subsequent editions.

Unless otherwise acknowledged, all photographs are the property of Scott Foresman, a division of Pearson Education.

Photo locators denoted as follows: Top (T), Center (C), Bottom (B), Left (L), Right (R), Background (Bkgd).

5 Getty Images; **32** (TR, TL) ©C Squared Studios/Getty Images, (CL, BR, CR) Getty Images, (BL) ©Spike Mafford/Getty Images; **33** (BL) Getty Images, (BR) ©Taxi/Getty Images; **45** Comstock Images; **63** ©Dex Image/Getty Images; **65** (CR) Getty Images, (CR) ©DK Images; **66** (TR) Getty Images; **67** (CR) ©Burke/Triolo/Jupiter Images, (T) ©Wolfgang Deuter/Zefa/Corbis, (BC, CL) Getty Images; **68** (C) ©Georg Gerster/Photo Researchers, Inc., (CL) Getty Images; **69** (C) ©Ken Lucas/Visuals Unlimited, (CR) Demetrio Carrasco/©DK Images; **70** Harry Taylor/©DK Images; **71** (C) Demetrio Carrasco/©DK Images, (T, BC) Getty Images, (CR) Harry Taylor/©DK Images; **72** (BL) Harry Taylor/©DK Images, (TL, BR) ©DK Images, (TR) Colin Keates/The Natural History Museum, London/©DK Images; **73** Colin Keates, The Natural History Museum, London/©DK Images; **74** ©Aldo Tutino/Art Resource, NY; **75** (CL) Colin Keates/The Natural History Museum, London/©DK Images, (C, BR) Harry Taylor/©DK Images, (B) ©Olivier Cirendini/Lonely Planet Images; **76** (TR) Colin Keates, The Natural History Museum, London/©DK Images, (C) AP/Wide World Photos; **77** (C) ©Buddy Mays/Corbis, (BR) ©Siede Preis/Getty Images; **85** (BC) ©Tom Bean/Corbis, (BR) ©Astrid & Hanns-Frieder Michler/Photo Researchers, Inc.; **87** (TC, TR) Getty Images, (CR) ©C Squared Studios/Getty Images; **88** ©Ariel Skelley/Corbis; **89** ©Masterfile Corporation; **90** (CL) ©Stockdisc/Getty Images, (C) ©C Squared Studios/Getty Images; **91** ©David McLain/Aurora/Getty Images; **92** (C) ©Macduff Everton/Getty Images, (TL) Getty Images; **93** (C) ©Yellow Dog Productions/Getty Images, (CR) Getty Images; **94** ©Daniel Bosler/Getty Images; **95** (C) Getty Images, (CL) ©Siede Preis/Getty Images; **96** ©C Squared Studios/Getty Images; **98** ©Kevin Dodge/Corbis; **99** ©Masterfile Royalty-Free; **100** ©Joseph Sohm/ChromoSohm Inc./Corbis; **101** Getty Images; **102** ©DAJ/Getty Images; **103** ©Masterfile Royalty-Free; **109** (BR) ©C Squared Studios/Getty Images, (BC) ©Stewart Cohen/Getty Images; **117** Getty Images; **135** ©Juniors Bildarchiv/Alamy; **159** Getty Images